…HERSTORY

MEMOIRS FROM DAUGHTERS TO MOTHERS AS THEIR MENTORS

Dr. Andrea Blue, Ph.D.

…HerStory

MEMOIRS

FROM DAUGHTERS

TO MOTHERS

AS THEIR MENTORS

By

Dr. Andrea Blue, Ph.D.

Doctor of Management in Organizational

Development and Change

Blue

P A T H W A Y S

ACKNOWLEDGMENTS

Writing this book has evoked countless emotions. In many ways, writing this book was like putting a puzzle together.

To my husband, Lawrence, thank you for supporting my inkling to be in solitude and do nothing but write this book. What a gift that time was to possess. Thanks, too, for your continued support of this project. I never want to forget this journey and how grateful that I am to have you in my life. I love you. True love always!

Encouragement from Mrs. Beatrice Thomas (Precious Mother); children (Keasha, Tony, Ashley, and Geraldetta (niece)); grandchildren (Nick and Brylin); all of my mentors, family, and friends; Colorado Technical University staff; editor; Gold Stars; proofreaders; haters; researchers; seminar and support groups; and therapists.

It was tough finding the title of this book. Many individuals contributed to the ideas until we landed on this one: ...*HerStory*. The title suggestions were hilarious. Thanks to everyone that shared their input. Finally, I settled on "...*HerStory*" (pronounced, hurstoree). What a blessing to write this book. I have had the opportunity to work with

many fantabulous individuals and outstanding people that
have contributed to this project!

– Dr. Blue

ABOUT THE AUTHOR

Experience

As a method of introduction, my name is *Dr. Andrea Marie Blue, Ph.D.*

For an introduction, my name is **Dr. Blue**, a native of Baldwin, Michigan (born and raised). I possess more than 15 years of experience in the areas of business, higher education, mentorship, philanthropy, and organizational management. As a service learner, I obtained my professional experience and academic credentials while working full time and attending college. This experience enabled me to effectively utilize the scholar-practitioner model to provide instruction and team-based learning to churches, colleges, universities, middle and high schools, nonprofit organizations, parents, and students. At present, I operate as the Chief Executive Officer and Founder of B & J Enterprises, LLC, where I am responsible for providing policy and guidance within the business. This business provides speaking engagements, team building activities, workshops, professional developments, student assemblies, and monthly lunch and learn occasions. These occasions will be held at the client's location or a scheduled location that is convenient for both the client and Blue Pathways. We focus on underprivileged and underrepresented populations.

Hobbies

When I am not teaching or providing mentorship with Blue Pathways, I enjoy spending time with family, traveling, and dining out. I try my best to be the finest me possible through love and light.

EDUCATION

Doctor of Management in Organizational Development and Higher Education Teaching and Learning - Colorado Technical University

Master of Science in Advanced Studies - Ferris State University

Master of Science in Career Technical Education – Ferris State University

Bachelors of Science – Business Administration – Ferris State University

Certificates:

- Advanced Project Management
- Online Adjunct Teaching
- Higher Education - Instructor Concentration
- Supervision
- Career Technical Education – Leadership Capstone
- Computer Information Systems – Database Management and Administration
- Speech Communication
- Office Systems Technology

Publications

EXPLORING MENTORING STRATEGIES NEEDED BY HIGHER EDUCATIONAL MANAGERS TO INCREASE STUDENT RETENTION RATES AND DECREASE DROPOUT RATES IN A HIGHER EDUCATION ORGANIZATION - MARCH 2018

FOREWORD

Sometimes, as daughters, we feel as opposites of our mothers, just like fire and ice. We believe that we do not have anything in common. As time progresses, we begin to realize that we may be more like our mothers as we get older than we dare to admit. Our mothers teach us about life rather it is good, bad, indifferent.

What is this book about?

Dr. Andrea Blue, Ph.D., is dedicated to transformation. This book is a tool that will be used to spark conversation about transforming lives through mentorship. Since the beginning of her career, Dr. Blue has included education/mentorship, entrepreneurship, life skills, organizational change and development, and women's issues as a means of working with all people from various walks of life. Her background is in education, business, management, and organizational development and change.

This book includes the stories of women that have been invited to write a letter to their mothers. This book is independently organized and will lead to future endeavors that surround mentorship. I am a huge fan of the determination, tenacity, and love for life that these women possess. They are appreciated for their methods of handling stress in life, and their letters are openly welcome to this project.

The women are writing letters to their mothers and want to share their stories with other women of all ages that may need a mentor. This project will be a valuable contribution to the research and findings that could lead to a greater public understanding of mentoring strategies used by higher educational managers to increase student retention rates and decrease student dropout rates in a higher education organization.

Some women are emotionally stuck at a young age and have a hard time moving beyond their younger years into adulthood because they have not shared their hearts with their mothers. You may not be sure how to write the letter or what to say, but some women have started the letters for you and shared their stories. Your story is your story, and it all starts by saying yes to a better life for you! Write the letter to your mother, whether she is here or not!

Where does this book take place?

This book will begin with a story of a little brown girl that grew up in a rural town. The little girl was raised as a strong, religious, hardworking, single, and divorced mother. The little girl loved and cherished her mother because she is her SHERO! She longed to be with her mother.

During the age of six, little girls are changing through social interactions, and their cognitive skills are developing. They are moving toward being more independent, both emotionally and intellectually. Little girls are observing and learning language and logic from their caretakers, which is usually the mother figure. As they are faced with choices, they find it difficult to make choices without the fear of disappointment of their caretaker.

At the tender age of six, young girls are craving affection and attention from their parents, teachers, and friends. Their feelings can be hurt very easily, which is a reflection of sensitivity. They crave an audience and praise, which can be a blow to their self-esteem when they are not acknowledged. There needs to be a sense of accomplishment or achievement.

At the age of six, young girls begin to lose their imagination. Their imaginary playmate goes away, and they depend more on pictures. At the age of six, young girls live directly through the lives of their mothers or female authority figures. At six, rules are the best thing ever. Order and structure are very important to them. If there is chaos, their world can be out of control. As a result, their mother can be their best friend, whether she is there or not, which can be both positive and negative.

When does this book take place?

This book is a continual piece of work. The book takes place around the world. These stories encompass women from all walks of life. Every story is written with heart, mind, and soul. This book will be used to support courses, workshops, professional developments, and lunch and learns that are focused on mentorship.

Why was this book written?

This book was written to encourage every little girl out there that can't find her voice but has a great deal to say. This book was written to help any mother, daughter, sister, friend, and lover understand the little six-year-old girl in all of us.

Some of our relationships are flawed, a work in progress, or beyond repair. It does not matter the stage of the relationship; it only matters that the relationship is …

How will this book add to research?

This book will be one of many that will be used to promote mentorship through education, career, entrepreneurship, and personal development.

– Dr. Andrea Blue, Ph.D.

INTRODUCTION

I guess you are wondering what makes me an expert to teach you about the importance of mentorship from birth until our last days on this earth. You may be wondering, "What the heck does she know about struggling and trying to figure it all out?" Well, I would want to know more about me as well. There are so many people in this world claiming that they have the answers and can solve problems of those that are hurting. They claim to know how to bring in money in "six" figures, and they are struggling themselves. You may want to know what makes people trustworthy when trust is not a requirement of gurus anymore.

I am an expert in the field of mentorship because I know the importance and value of having a dedicated mentor in your life. I know the ins and outs of what it takes to complete dreams and goals and get a business off the ground but not understanding exactly how to get it done. I understand the necessary measures that must be taken as it relates to difficult decisions, struggling financially, being a single parent and wanting more out of life, and building a business. I know about the tough conversations that must be held with children and a spouse to discuss the goals for my future that may include more sacrifice from all. I understand the importance of working a 9–5 while planning and building for the future, all the while wanting to be somewhere else. You must realize that when you put the extra work into building your goals, it is important to have a mentor that can assist with the process beyond prayer, yourself, family, and friends.

I have been in the business of mentorship since 2000. I have worked with so many different colleges, universities, nonprofits, students, parents, organizational leaders, churches, and individuals that were not good stewards of their time and putting a plan in place for their future. I have built relationships over the years with individuals that I have grown to love. I have been nominated and won many awards, and I have a great deal to be proud of throughout my lifetime. God is good! My business, B & J Enterprises, LLC, has been nominated for awards and has been asked to be a part of many discussions. We often sit at the head of the table leading these discussions. I am not being boastful but being grateful. These awards were not won alone and were the result of a great deal of hard work from those that were in the struggle with me.

I have been through so many trials and tribulations being a mentor and entrepreneur. Family and friends have turned their backs on me, but I never lost faith because I know that God has a purpose in my life. I have lost my mother and best friend, and there have been times that I had no money to show. The mentor that I thought I could turn to was not present and criticized the work that was done and never believed in me. I have learned so much through mistakes. I am not perfect now, but if I can help someone avoid the mistakes, heartache, money losses that I experienced by providing mentorship and building an empire, I would do it all again.

The reason that I shared this information with you is that I want you to know Mentorship Matters! Your goals are achievable with a plan. You may think that you can run a business, sell products, write a book, or set any goal and achieve it without a mentor, but you are sadly mistaken. I know from experience that a mentor is important to the process. You will be able to overcome the struggles that come in your life as you journey to complete the plan in action. You will be able to stay focused on courage. This is not to say that you will not have bad days and feel low, but a mentor will be there to push you through the hard times despite it all. The work that we do does not end with us; it is only the beginning.

There are risks that you must take, but I hope that this book will help you get closer to your goals and dreams. You are more than a conqueror, and you are capable of making your life happen. No one is coming to save you. It is important to make a plan, write it down and put it into action. This is your book. Write in it! Take notes! Use it as a guide with your mentor. If you do not have a mentor, plan to attend one of my dynamic, fun-filled workshops at a location near you with Blue Pathways. Reflect on your goals and where you desire to be in the next 30, 60, 90 days. At the end of each chapter, I have included an opportunity for you to reflect on the information in the chapters. A plan is the only way that you will see your vision come true. A mentor can walk this path with you.

I will share my story with you as you are on this journey with me to create your own plan. You will learn a great deal in the process. This will not be a quick journey but a purposeful one. Where you are today is not your final destination. Dr. Blue uses Blue Pathways Educational Mentorship Services as the vehicle to drive individuals to their success. Will you join me on this ride? You got this!

– **Dr. Blue**

DEDICATION

To Lawrence Blue, Jr., and all of the individuals that have believed in me through this journey; I dedicate this book to you. I send a special dedication to anyone that lacked educational mentors before, while, and after secondary and post-secondary education. Hold fast to truthfulness, morality, hard work, liberality, and compassion and lend a helping hand to those that are walking in your shoes.

This book is dedicated to the writers of the stories Ashley, Latesa, Leola, Lesli, Angel, Stormie, and all the mothers that have changed and shaped our lives through love, misunderstandings, unsolved mysteries, or unacknowledged hurt.

This book is dedicated to girls young and old that have struggled, are struggling, or will struggle with their relationships with their mothers. I understand your pain, and you are not alone.

TABLE OF CONTENTS

Acknowledgments i

About the Author iii

Foreword vii

Introduction xi

Dedication xv

Chapter 1:   Humble Beginnings in Life… 5

Chapter 2:   Memories from A Young Age Can Cause
              Pain … 20

Chapter 3:   My Mother, My Rock… 33

Chapter 4:   My Past Is Not My Future… 47

Chapter 5:   Difficult Relationships Are Lessons Taught…62

Chapter 6:   The Love of A Mother Conquers All… 77

Chapter 7:   Mothers Hurt Too… 89

Chapter 8:   The Loss of Our Mothers… 103

Chapter 9:   Forgiveness! The Reason We Should Forgive
              and Never Forget… 118

Chapter 10: The Next Chapter… 131

Chapter 11: How Can I Make A Difference? 133

Introduction

Chapter 1

Chapter 2

Chapter 3

Chapter 4

Chapter 5

Chapter 6

Chapter 7

Chapter 8

Chapter 9

Chapter 10

Chapter 11

LET'S REFLECT...

REFLECTION

As she stood there staring straight ahead, looking at all the imperfections on her face, all the while pushing her long, thick, black wavy hair to the side, wondering why HER hair was not straight, she attempted to smile and looked at her teeth and noticed that HER teeth were a little big and crooked, all the while never moving her head aside to look away at her face, hair, and teeth.

She began to tell herself all of the things that she needed to change about her appearance, features, and her past. She never stopped to realize that she had just overcome one of the hardest storms in her life; where she was losing herself while trying to save others.

She began to look at herself and slowly realize that she had made it through the storm and was well on her way. She began to become thankful for HER face because some are born without noses, eyes, and ears. She began to run her fingers through her hair and thank God in heaven that the hereditary bald spot skipped her generation.

HER outlook changed, and her teeth looked new, and she realized that the HER that she was degrading was me; I was staring at my own reflection, criticizing God's creation.

3

How dare I criticize such a beautiful masterpiece? God, please forgive me.

For she is God's child, and the REFLECTION is in HIS image; perfectly constructed.

– Dr. Andrea Blue, Ph.D.

CHAPTER 1

HUMBLE BEGINNINGS IN LIFE...

DR. BLUE'S HUMBLE BEGINNINGS IN LIFE

As a little girl, the world seemed so huge. It seemed as though life was a movie, and things around were happening to me, and I was so confused. In the movie, I was the star but never in control of the camera. I can recall walking and talking to people around me and feeling invisible; however, the camera was still rolling. I never told anyone.

He Hurt Me

I remember lying in my bed, and a big black man would pick me up out of my bed and straddle me on his lap, facing him. I remember never looking up. I don't remember what took place; I just knew that it felt immoral. I remember him putting me back in my bed and walking out the darkroom into the dark living room. However, the moon was shining through the big picture window, and I could remember thinking, "Dear God …" I soon stopped talking and feeling the same about life. Things were a little darker for me. I mentioned these episodes, and I was told I was lying. I was five years old.

Walking ...

I could remember the camera rolling again, and the star was in action again. Her skin was sticky and sweaty from the heat of the sun. The sun was beating her face and back as if it were 1000 degrees on the summer day. However, she did not care because she was on a mission. Her little black shiny shoes with the Velcro strap were making her feet sweat. The dust from the dusty road was apparent that she did not put any Vaseline on those shoes today. However, she knew that the rule was not to be near the construction site. However, she knew that she was safe because HE was with her, and she always felt safe with HIM. He was normally red-faced because his skin was so light, but his skin was glowing today. He saw her walking along the path to go to the new house where construction was being conducted to build the "new house"; he grabbed her hand and led her into the construction site. As they walked into the location with no door, they could smell the fresh-cut wood; the house was steamy from the cut wood and the steam of the sun beaming through every window. The "new house" was on its way. As they walked into the location and stepped upon the wooden plank because there was no floor, he looked around and said: "She will love this place. Yes, Peaches will love this place." He held my hand, and we walked all the way to the back, and he held my hand so tight and lifted me up straight in the air as the plank on the floor flipped up. If he had not lifted me up, I may have fallen to the ground under the new house onto the nails that were sticking up out of the new wood. I looked upon his beautiful face and wondered what had happened because he never was rough or even spoke above a whisper. He said, "Baby girl," because that was what he called me, "do you see that shiny nail sticking up right there?" I said nothing because I knew that he saved my life and a possible trip to the far-away hospital. So, I put a strong grip on his hand as to say thank you. We headed out the door from the back of the house back into the blazing sun. I couldn't wait to tell my family what had just happened and how beautiful the house was. So, I saw her, and I was so excited, and I began to tell the story all out of breath and full of excitement ... she said, "That could not have happened because he has been dead for almost 4 months." She also added, "Don't tell anybody else that because they will think you are crazy." Oh, well, I guess I should not tell anybody about the time he helped me find my Barbie that was under my bed either ... oh well, I will never forget that long hot summer day and our walk into the "new house."

After the New House Was Built

Living in the new house was awesome. I was six years old and watching my mother, and it was the highlight of my life. I would watch her every move. She worked outside the home and woke up at 4 a.m. to drive 20 minutes to work; she cooked dinner, completed her crossword puzzles, and drank her coffee with a saucer under it. On Sundays, church was always on the agenda. My mother sang in the choir, and I knew every song and was delighted to hear her sing. She mentored without even knowing it; my mother, my Shero.

Questions

1. We know that situations and circumstances occur without our control. How can you use your humble beginning experience as an opportunity to benefit your future?

_____

_____

_____

_____

_____

_____

_____

_____

_____

_____

_____

_____

...HerStory
MEMOIRS FROM DAUGHTERS TO MOTHERS AS THEIR MENTORS

_____

_____

_____

_____

_____

_____

_____

_____

_____

_____

_____

_____

_____

_____

_____

_____

_____

_____

_____

_____

_____

_____

_____

_____

_____

_____

_____

_____

_____

_____

2. How can you use your humble beginnings to show your
   passion to benefit your future?

   _____

   _____

   _____

   _____

   _____

   _____

   _____

   _____

   _____

   _____

   _____

   _____

   _____

   _____

_____

_____

_____

_____

_____

_____

_____

_____

_____

_____

_____

_____

_____

_____

_____

_____

_____

_____

_____

_____

_____

_____

_____

_____

_____

_____

_____

_____

_____

_____

_____

_____

3. If you are struggling to move from your past, what abilities can you use to move beyond your past and forward to your next strides?

_____

_____

_____

_____

_____

_____

_____

_____

_____

_____

_____

_____

_____

_____

_____

_____

_____

_____

_____

_____

_____

_____

_____

_____

_____

_____

_____

_____

_____

_____

_____

_____

_____

_____

_____

_____

_____

_____

_____

_____

_____

_____

_____

_____

CHAPTER 2

MEMORIES FROM A YOUNG AGE CAN CAUSE PAIN …

MEMORIES FROM A YOUNG AGE CAN CAUSE PAIN

Dear Mommy,

The definition of a mentor states: "A mentor may share with a mentee (or protégé) information about his or her own career path, as well as provide guidance, motivation, emotional support, and role modeling." A.K.A. my mother! At a young age, I found it hard for your words to stick; it wasn't until I got older they started to register. Your guidance and wisdom is never unnoticed and is greatly appreciated. I'm writing this memoir to you. I aspire to be half the mother you have been to me and my siblings.

Memories for me at the age of six were vague, but one clear thing was the consistent love I received. During the young age of six, you and my father were preparing for a divorce, and although I don't remember much, I remember you held me so tight during this time, and you protected and made me feel so loved. Physically, you knew you couldn't replace my father, but your love was definitely close, and you did the ABSOLUTE best you could, and I thank you for that. Your bravery and courage have definitely molded me into the woman I am today.

Being the youngest child, you held me tight; you protected me and interfered with any possible harm, and I didn't understand that was love until I got older. Not every child has a mother that cares so much, that she understands so much and loves so much. The opportunities you open for us at such a young age gave me the confidence that the possibilities were endless. Your support will always stick with me. You always say, "Girl, you can be whatever you want to be as long as you do your best," and my favorite: "Did you do your best? Well, that's all you can do, baby." Some children don't have this support/understanding or any support at all, and I'm so grateful and thankful I did.

Mom, thank you for your guidance, your wisdom, love, and support. Your strides, sacrifices, courage, and bravery motivate me every day. I want you to know that when I do have children, I hope to show them the same love and encouragement that you have shown me.

Questions

1. Relationships are different from our mothers for each of us. What are we placing in front of us as a compass to move us from today and into tomorrow?

_____

_____

_____

_____

_____

_____

_____

_____

_____

_____

_____

_____

...HerStory

MEMOIRS FROM DAUGHTERS TO MOTHERS AS THEIR MENTORS

_____

_____

_____

_____

_____

_____

_____

_____

_____

_____

_____

_____

_____

_____

_____

_____

...*HerStory*

MEMOIRS FROM DAUGHTERS TO MOTHERS AS THEIR MENTORS

_____

_____

_____

_____

_____

_____

_____

_____

_____

_____

_____

_____

_____

_____

_____

2. How will your compass help you in the future?

_____

_____

_____

_____

_____

_____

_____

_____

_____

_____

_____

_____

_____

_____

...HerStory
MEMOIRS FROM DAUGHTERS TO MOTHERS AS THEIR MENTORS

_____

_____

_____

_____

_____

_____

_____

_____

_____

_____

_____

_____

_____

_____

_____

...*HerStory*
MEMOIRS FROM DAUGHTERS TO MOTHERS AS THEIR MENTORS

_____

_____

_____

_____

_____

_____

_____

_____

_____

_____

_____

_____

_____

_____

_____

_____

_____

3. Who is your accountability partner? What is the plan that you both have set for the next 3 months?

_____

_____

_____

_____

_____

_____

_____

_____

_____

_____

_____

_____

_____

_____

…HerStory

MEMOIRS FROM DAUGHTERS TO MOTHERS AS THEIR MENTORS

_____

_____

_____

_____

_____

_____

_____

_____

_____

_____

_____

_____

_____

_____

_____

_____

_____

_____

_____

_____

_____

_____

_____

_____

_____

_____

_____

_____

_____

_____

_____

_____

_____

_____

CHAPTER 3

MY MOTHER, MY ROCK...

MY MOTHER, MY ROCK

On October 9th, 2017, my mother was rushed to the hospital due to her sugar being 1,567. She wasn't aware that she was diabetic. She was in ICU for 3 days and a regular hospital room for 3 more days. She doesn't remember the first two days, but I sure do. My mother had no clue who I was, and that was the scariest moment in my life. My mom was a diabetic, and I didn't know it. She was on the verge of going into a diabetic coma. She was rushed to the hospital. After a lot of tests and a 6-day stay, we were told that she was a diabetic, and luckily, we got her to the hospital when we did.

She has been my mom and dad for as long as I can remember; my dad died when I was three. So, after all the doctor's appointments, different medications, and all the ambulance calls due to her sugar dropping too low, we finally got a hold on everything, and my mom says, "Thank you for all your love and support."

My response was, "No need for thanks; I'm just doing what my mother taught me. I will ALWAYS love you with all my heart. I thank you for ALWAYS having my back, no matter what right, wrong, or indifferent. I love you for guiding me in the right direction that leads me to be the woman that I am today. I love you for doing everything in your power to make sure that I had everything that I needed or wanted, even when I didn't understand the extent that you had to go to. I am honored that GOD saw fit to make you my mother. I love that we have a bond that most people dream of having with their mother or daughter, and I wouldn't trade it for anything in the world. I love you to the moon and back and would kill a brick for you."

She is fine now. She is still a diabetic, but she took her situation very seriously and changed her eating habits as well as I to support her, and now she doesn't have to take insulin anymore just the pill and they are working on cutting that out as well.

My mom has been my mentor because she always goes above and beyond in anything that she has done. I have instilled my childhood and the way she raised me in my two children. My mom is a very kind-hearted individual; if she has it, and you need it, then it's yours. My mom is the most supportive person that I know. Anything that I was involved in as a child, a teenager, a college student, even an adult, she has been right by my side. She has also done the same with my children. If I call, she is right there. If I don't call, she is still right there. My mom is my everything and the greatest teacher in the world. I love her beyond words.

Questions

1. Stop and think about your mother for a moment. What are some of the words that were used to encourage your dreams or to cause you to reflect on being different than her?

_____

_____

_____

_____

_____

_____

_____

_____

_____

_____

_____

_____

_____

_____

_____

_____

_____

_____

_____

_____

_____

_____

_____

_____

_____

_____

_____

_____

_____

_____

_____

MEMOIRS FROM DAUGHTERS TO MOTHERS AS THEIR MENTORS

_____

_____

_____

_____

_____

_____

_____

_____

_____

_____

_____

_____

_____

_____

2. What words are you using today that cause harm or encouragement to others?

_____

_____

_____

_____

_____

_____

_____

_____

_____

_____

_____

_____

_____

_____

_____

_____

_____

_____

_____

_____

_____

_____

_____

_____

_____

_____

_____

_____

_____

_____

_____

_____

_____

_____

_____

_____

_____

_____

_____

_____

_____

_____

_____

_____

_____

_____

_____

3. What steps can you take to correct or continue those words to create a positive outlook for your future and those that you love?

_____

_____

_____

_____

_____

_____

_____

_____

_____

_____

_____

_____

_____

_____

_____

_____

_____

_____

_____

_____

_____

_____

_____

_____

_____

_____

_____

_____

_____

_____

_____

_____

_____

_____

_____

_____

_____

_____

_____

_____

_____

_____

CHAPTER 4

MY PAST
IS **NOT**
MY FUTURE...

MY PAST IS NOT MY FUTURE

Dear Momma,

Somebody told me to write you a letter and tell you what I have been too scared to tell you:

I am 6 years old. I am in the first grade. I don't like going to that school; the big girls try to beat me up. One girl tried to pull my slip off me. My big sister told her to stop and leave me alone. Every day she wants to hurt me. I hold on to my sister's dress tail everywhere she goes. When I don't want to go to school, she takes me in there anyway. The big girls didn't like my dresses and wanted to fight me. The kids don't like me, and some won't play with me, but this one boy plays with me on the swing and merry-go-round. He is nice. I am scared all the time. At school, I liked the plays I would do with my sister; it was fun, and I like saying the poems. I remembered them just like my teacher told me. You dress me so pretty and come to see us act. I remember, and you said I did well. You let me write and draw pictures. I remember you draw pictures, and I want to draw and write just like you, and you don't fuss at me, and you would help with my letters.

I liked my big brother and wanted to go with him, so I would get in his car, and he would take me with him to the lake and the skating rink. Then he would take me to his house. He taught me how to French kiss. He said it was okay. When I got home, I was scared to tell you because I didn't want to get a whooping 'cause I wanted to go with him. I don't like whooping. I am sorry I didn't ask you. I wanted to tell you how my sister and some other big boys that came over to our house would put their fingers in me; I was scared, so I didn't tell you. I didn't want you to be mad at me. I thought I would get a whooping if I told you, even when she did it, and you were in our room when we were in bed. She would make me do it to her. One day at school, I saw a boy being mean to her. He had his arm behind her back, and he dressed up when he saw me. I ran away and went back to the school. I wanted to tell you, but I don't know why I didn't tell anybody. I thought that was why she was sick and had to go to the hospital. I wish I knew how to tell you and how much I missed her. I would cry because no one was there to stop the big girls from picking on me. I missed you when you would go to be with her at the hospital. I liked it when you would come home and cook and put the food in the car, and Daddy would drive us to the hospital to see her. It would take so long; Daddy would stop at the park, and we would have a picnic. The food would be so good; I loved your food. We couldn't go in to see her. I didn't know why, but she would come to the window; it was so high I couldn't see her much. I didn't know how to ask you questions or to and tell you how I felt. I loved it when you would sit me on your lap and hug me; it felt good. I remember she came home one time before she died, and she was so skinny. She didn't talk, and she didn't do anything to me then. I loved my sister and my big brother; he left too and got married, and I felt I had no one to love me then. I didn't believe you loved me even, though you said it. I was scared of you, and I thought you didn't believe me. When I did tell you something, you would make me work all the time.

Remember, when we were at home, I used to go to my room and play and sing in the dark all by myself, but you scared me; you knocked at the door, and when I opened it, all I saw was that white stuff on your face. I was screaming for my momma and beating on you. I thought you were a monster after me, but you sat me on your lap and told me you are my mom and that you loved me. It took me a long time to believe you, but I did; however, I still couldn't go in the dark anymore. There were so many things I wanted to tell you, but I was scared, or I felt I shouldn't bother you. I was so scared all the time. I don't know why I felt like I was going to get a whooping all the time, but you didn't whoop me like the other kids. So I would just do the work you told me to do.

I guess I didn't know about heroes, or you being special, but what I did know: you took care of us all. I didn't understand you were hurting and grieving over the loss of your mother and now a daughter. I remember hearing you cry sometimes. I loved you, and I am so glad to write this letter to you. If I could tell another girl anything, I would say, "Tell your mom what others do and say to you." Grown people would say mean things to me, but I didn't tell my mom. Momma, you had a lot of children and a husband to take care of, and you were hurting too, but you looked out for me, and I didn't understand it that way.

Questions

1. Difficult relationships with our mothers can make or break us. Do you view your relationship with your mother as a failure?

_____

_____

_____

_____

_____

_____

_____

_____

_____

_____

_____

_____

_____

_____

_____

_____

_____

_____

_____

_____

_____

_____

_____

_____

_____

_____

_____

_____

_____

_____

_____

_____

_____

_____

_____

_____

_____

_____

_____

_____

_____

_____

_____

_____

_____

2. What does a successful relationship with your mother look like to you?

_____

_____

_____

_____

_____

_____

_____

_____

_____

_____

_____

_____

_____

_____

MEMOIRS FROM DAUGHTERS TO MOTHERS AS THEIR MENTORS

_____

_____

_____

_____

_____

_____

_____

_____

_____

_____

_____

_____

_____

_____

_____

_____

...HerStory

MEMOIRS FROM DAUGHTERS TO MOTHERS AS THEIR MENTORS

_____

_____

_____

_____

_____

_____

_____

_____

_____

_____

_____

_____

_____

_____

_____

_____

3. What situations do you consider unreconciled with your mother? What happened?

_____

_____

_____

_____

_____

_____

_____

_____

_____

_____

_____

_____

_____

_____

_____

_____

_____

_____

_____

_____

_____

_____

_____

_____

_____

_____

_____

_____

_____

_____

…HerStory
MEMOIRS FROM DAUGHTERS TO MOTHERS AS THEIR MENTORS

_____

_____

_____

_____

_____

_____

_____

_____

_____

_____

_____

_____

_____

_____

_____

_____

_____

CHAPTER 5

DIFFICULT RELATIONSHIPS ARE LESSONS TAUGHT...

DIFFICULT RELATIONSHIPS ARE LESSONS TAUGHT

A letter to my Mom ...

At times, we had a difficult relationship ... But you have done so much for me in my lifetime, and I really appreciate you. You still supported me even when you clearly did not understand my decisions or agree with them. You made it clear over the years how many of my decisions have hurt your heart. So much of the time, you took the way I lived my life *personally* like I was trying to hurt you. For me, it was critical I lived my life and did what made me happy. It took me several years to come to the conclusion that I needed your "Love," but I did not need your "Approval."

There are so many things that you have impressed upon me in my lifetime that you may not even be aware of. You taught me integrity and how to treat people with fairness and respect. You taught me how important it is to research your options and the steps it takes to get where you want to be. You taught me to do my best at all times—because people are always watching, and you never know where that can take you. You taught me that taking risks is okay—as

63

long as you are willing to take on any possible results. You taught me to finish what I started and to not leave loose ends. You taught me to be careful who I love and let into my life ... Leading me to live by trusting only those who prove to be trustworthy.

Over the years, I have watched you run a household, build 2 homes, buy and sell many properties, be involved with several business dealings, charity organizations, plan and organize amazing parties and events, and be a supportive partner to friends and family. You always made it clear you had your own life to live, and although you invited me to share it with you at times, we never really had a mother-daughter relationship like so many others do. I shared parts of my life with you but also kept many parts of my life a secret due to being afraid of disappointing you. I have always known I was not really the daughter you wanted. I actually thought I was adopted for many years because our thought processes about people and life were so different, and I never understood it. But I also know you were very proud of me at times ... Not because you ever told me; only because you would write it in the cards you would mail me.

Our communication and visiting time was pretty consistent. I leaned on you for support during rough times and enjoyed including you during times of celebration. We lived 2.5 hours apart—and I visited you 1x/month, and you came to visit me during times of celebration or important events. I called you 1–2x a week for most of my life unless you were sick then I called more than that. I got married 2x, and due to my partner's decisions, you chose not to attend, which was not a disappointment to me; it was more of a relief. So when I say we did not have a normal "mother-daughter" relationship ... this is an example. You were always there for my two daughters and very involved in making sure they had what they needed to be happy and successful in life. Your help was greatly appreciated in helping me build strong daughters.

You taught me about how to be a good mom ... and also things I didn't want to be as a mom. I had to teach my daughters how to love and respect a parent even if you don't see things the same way. That took years to teach and to be honest, I am still working on them even now. They struggled with how to keep peace with you when they did not agree with you or when you spoke negatively about me or other people. They struggled with how I wanted to keep a relationship with you when there were so many issues where we did not agree. I constantly advised my girls, "Although I do not agree with Grandma on many issues, I still love her and want her in my life. She will not change and that is okay. Everyone has the right to believe what they want as long as they are not hurting anyone." Every month, on the way to Grandma's, we would have "The Talk," which consisted of: "If politics, social issues, religion, gay rights, abortion or world issues come up in our discussion ... Please just change the subject."

I watched you give to so many people over my life without strings attached ... But when you gave to me, I many times felt an obligation to you (like I owed you).

Questions

1. What makes you afraid to revisit the past or future as it relates to stepping into a new you?

_____

_____

_____

_____

_____

_____

_____

_____

_____

_____

_____

_____

_____

…HerStory
MEMOIRS FROM DAUGHTERS TO MOTHERS AS THEIR MENTORS

_____

_____

_____

_____

_____

_____

_____

_____

_____

_____

_____

_____

_____

_____

_____

MEMOIRS FROM DAUGHTERS TO MOTHERS AS THEIR MENTORS

_____

_____

_____

_____

_____

_____

_____

_____

_____

_____

_____

_____

_____

_____

_____

2. Let's reflect on our last conversation with our mothers. What is preventing you from moving forward? What is holding you back from taking risks with new relationships?

_____

_____

_____

_____

_____

_____

_____

_____

_____

_____

_____

_____

_____

_____

_____

_____

_____

_____

_____

_____

_____

_____

_____

_____

_____

_____

_____

_____

_____

_____

_____

_____

_____

_____

_____

_____

_____

_____

_____

_____

_____

_____

_____

_____

_____

3. What steps can you take to recover from the past lessons and confront your fears and hurt from the past?

_____

_____

_____

_____

_____

_____

_____

_____

_____

_____

_____

_____

_____

_____

...HerStory
MEMOIRS FROM DAUGHTERS TO MOTHERS AS THEIR MENTORS

_____

_____

_____

_____

_____

_____

_____

_____

_____

_____

_____

_____

_____

_____

_____

_____

_____

_____

_____

_____

_____

_____

_____

_____

_____

_____

_____

_____

_____

_____

_____

CHAPTER 6

THE LOVE OF A MOTHER CONQUERS ALL...

THE LOVE OF A MOTHER
CONQUERS ALL

Dear Mom,

I love you. I love you because you are determined, fierce, strong, bold—and most importantly, a lover of God. You are the reason why I strive to perfect my craft. You are the reason why I am who I've become; determined, fierce, strong, bold, and a lover of God. I often think back on how I could have done things differently. The more and more I embrace how things are, the better I've become at critiquing it to make things better for my five children. It isn't easy being a mom, and I wrote my own guidebook. I've paved the way for them to learn from my mistakes so that they don't have to walk down the path I did. I know now that the things I've been through have made me the person that I am today. I love being an entrepreneur, and I don't think I would have aced it if it wasn't for your direction from early on. Thank you, Mom, and I love you.

Questions

1. Where would you like to be in the next 2 years as it relates to your future self?

_____

_____

_____

_____

_____

_____

_____

_____

_____

_____

_____

_____

_____

_____

_____

_____

_____

_____

_____

_____

_____

_____

_____

_____

_____

_____

_____

_____

_____

...HerStory

MEMOIRS FROM DAUGHTERS TO MOTHERS AS THEIR MENTORS

_____

_____

_____

_____

_____

_____

_____

_____

_____

_____

_____

_____

_____

_____

_____

_____

2. Are there any relationships that you need to correct with people that are preventing you from moving forward? Write down the names of the individuals.

_____

_____

_____

_____

_____

_____

_____

_____

_____

_____

_____

_____

_____

_____

_____

_____

_____

_____

_____

_____

_____

_____

_____

_____

_____

_____

_____

_____

_____

_____

_____

_____

_____

_____

_____

_____

_____

_____

_____

_____

_____

_____

_____

_____

3. The names of the people from above can prevent you from moving forward. Write down their names and set a plan by adding dates to the calendar to contact them to have a conversation. It's always great when we start conversations.

_____

_____

_____

_____

_____

_____

_____

_____

_____

_____

_____

...HerStory
MEMOIRS FROM DAUGHTERS TO MOTHERS AS THEIR MENTORS

_____

_____

_____

_____

_____

_____

_____

_____

_____

_____

_____

_____

_____

_____

_____

CHAPTER 7

MOTHERS
HURT
TOO...

HUMAN MOTHER

It's always an interesting exploration when I'm asked to think back to times in my childhood, the times when I was the tiny cute brown girl with beautiful hair and a big smile. Rainbow Brite and She-Ra were my favorite TV programs, and my mom was still at an age where she wore stilettos and fancy jewelry. Today I'm a 37-year-old doctor and a mother myself, and I'm charmed by the opportunity to look back at the memories of the mother I knew when I was 6.

My mother is an absolutely beautiful creamy colored human who has a mix between a black man and a white woman. My grandfather was of Native American and Southern African American descent, and my grandmother was a blonde hair blue-eyed German. Together they created this wonderful creamy colored human I call my mother! My mom was always a curvy woman who was highly fashionable, all while struggling to make ends meet. I can just remember being 6 years old and knowing that it was very important for my mother to go to work so that we had money to live, but it was also important for her to have a little bit of style. I can remember even at 6 years old watching the struggle for that to play out. How to work and earn and provide and also cherish and honor your own youth? I thought my mom was the best thing in the world and the safest place I could ever be. She was loaded with strength and decisiveness, but I think the thing I remember the most is self-sacrifice. My mother always did what needed to be done. And even then, I remember thinking, *I wonder if this is to her detriment.* I just always wanted my mom to be as happy as she was making me. I always wanted her to have more money so that I could see her relax a little bit and really enjoy her stilettos. Even at 6, I remember thinking, *I wish I could provide more freedom for you or just make it easier.* That strength and determination and willingness to do what had to be done characterized the woman I met at 6 and who I still know today. It may sound a bit messier all over the place, but here was this woman, just another human being who now had a child to take care of, also trying to embrace her own youth; she was trapped with her own issues, as each of us; she was the most loving, caring, and supportive woman that I had in my life! That is the definition of a life well-lived and humanity. I had a mother who was absolutely human, and that is the best thing I think she could have ever given to me. I had all the love and all of the hugs, and I was extremely spoiled because I used to get nightly head massages to help me fall asleep, and then there was the one time she brought home my very own Michael Jackson record player!!!! The point is that I was fortunate enough to have a mother and to remember a mother who is imperfectly perfectly human, who sacrificed for me and who was just this magical unicorn of a woman! As I look at my mother today as a 37-year-old mother myself, I see her quite differently. She is still fierce and determined and does what needs to be done, but today, she is wisdom in motion. She's a legacy that I have the opportunity to stand on the shoulders of going forward. She's exactly who she was when I was 6; today, I just know how all of her humanness has created the wisdom and beauty that she gets to be today.

Questions

MEMOIRS FROM DAUGHTERS TO MOTHERS AS THEIR MENTORS

1. What is your passion?

_____

_____

_____

_____

_____

_____

_____

_____

_____

_____

_____

_____

_____

_____

_____

_____

_____

_____

_____

_____

_____

_____

_____

_____

_____

_____

_____

_____

_____

_____

_____

_____

_____

_____

_____

_____

_____

_____

_____

_____

_____

_____

_____

_____

_____

2. How can your passion be used to develop steps to be better in 6 months than you are today as it relates to relationships, business, career, education, and professional development?

_____

_____

_____

_____

_____

_____

_____

_____

_____

_____

_____

_____

_____

_____

_____

_____

_____

_____

_____

_____

_____

_____

_____

_____

_____

_____

_____

_____

_____

_____

_____

_____

_____

_____

_____

_____

_____

_____

_____

_____

_____

_____

_____

3. Plan for the future! Start adding dates to your calendar when you will work on your personal plan for the next 30, 60, and 90 days to add your passion to your goals in life.

…HerStory

MEMOIRS FROM DAUGHTERS TO MOTHERS AS THEIR MENTORS

_____

_____

_____

_____

_____

_____

_____

_____

_____

_____

_____

_____

_____

_____

_____

_____

_____

_____

_____

_____

_____

_____

_____

_____

_____

_____

_____

_____

_____

_____

_____

_____

_____

CHAPTER 8
THE LOSS OF OUR MOTHERS...

MOTHERLESS CHILD

Dear Mama, what an amazing mentor, leader, and confidant you have been to me over the years as a young adult. I remember our talks and prayers at 6 a.m. in the morning. I would expect those calls because I knew that they were coming like clockwork, whether it felt like prayer or not. For that, I will be eternally grateful. Those prayers brought me through so many areas of my life that were dark. However, as a little girl, I often wondered where my mama was and why she did not take me with her.

As a young girl, I remember that my life was very unclear. I had so many questions, and my main questions were "Where is Mama?" and "Is Mama my real mother?" These questions always loomed in the back of my mind because I wondered why I was not living with you. Why did I live with family members that did not feed me for days, did not purchase clothes or toys for me, but I lived in someone else's home, borrowing and using their children's things? Life was not amazing, but I was alive, had shelter, and I always knew that my big brother would be there to protect me when he came home on the weekends on leave from the Army. Providing safety and protection was important.

There were so many situations that took place that was unexplained. It was like I was in a movie. I was the STAR but not in control of the camera. I can recall walking and talking to people and being invisible. I would watch your every move. I wanted to be noticed and gain your attention. You were not a hugger when I was younger.

After church, you changed clothes, came in the house, and pots and pans were pulled out and filled with plenty of goodness. The house was always full of people, laughter, fights, and plenty of screaming. There were always plenty of conversations about making the right choices.

You were my mentor and taught me about resilience, determination, being tough, and faith. Your faith in God was impeccable. Mama, I know that you believed in God, and good things would happen, whether times were easy or hard. Mama, you were always on your way to church, work, or school. You were determined to be more than the average woman living in a small town raising eleven children.

I know that it had to be hard to birth thirteen children and lose one to cancer. After you left this earth, another one of your children left right behind you. She could not take the pain of your being gone either. Since you are our mentor, all of your children have an achieved goal, joining the armed forces, attending college, graduated from college, earned doctoral degrees from college, and run successful businesses. We watched you strive to go to work every day of the week, attend church, and graduate from college. What more could a mentor offer?

If your children are not the first partakers of your fruit while watching your life, then you need to get it together. Mama, you showed me how to get it together before sharing my story with the world. You groomed me to be the first partaker of my own fruit (children) for the world.

Some of your children grabbed onto your teachings, strict instruction, and harsh words to guide us toward goals. Others did not produce their own fruit (goals), and their trees did not produce good fruit. The seed from the fruit you plant should continue to produce more fruit. Some fruit has fallen to the ground and is dead or is starting to die. I have so many questions.

As a young girl, you were not there for me to ask the tough questions. I often found myself asking others, and they would give me the answer they wanted me to have from their perspective. However, you always taught us to research the information when we were unsure. To this day, I take the word of no one without looking up the facts to confirm. Trust has become a huge factor for me. I trust no one.

Mama, when you left me in 2013 and went to sleep, my whole world flipped upside down. All the memories of my childhood, laughter, tears, visits, hugs, kisses, prayers, and quiet times of sitting next to each other hip to hip meant the world to me. I have no regrets! I know that you did your best! I know that you loved me! I am glad that you are my mother and mentor. You have taught me so much over the years. I miss you every day and thank God above that when you left this earth, opportunities were not missed to tell you how much I love you and appreciate you. I wake up every day, wondering how I will go on without you here to call me at 6 a.m. and pray with me. Now, I know it is up to me to live a life that is planned for me. I will not try to live your life but work hard to be the best me possible.

Mama, thank you for showing me what it means to be there for your children. The love and attention that you could not show me, you poured into my children. You were there for every birth, and I will never forget it. I have no regrets and will always raise my hand to God above in gratitude for the mother that is mine.

Mama, thank you for being a great mentor to me, my children, and to all that came across your path. You will forever be missed, loved, and appreciated.

Questions

1. What is your definition of a successful future?

_____

_____

_____

_____

_____

_____

_____

_____

_____

_____

_____

_____

_____

_____

_____

_____

_____

_____

_____

_____

_____

_____

_____

_____

_____

_____

_____

_____

_____

_____

_____

_____

_____

_____

_____

_____

_____

_____

_____

_____

_____

_____

_____

_____

_____

_____

2. What are your next steps toward a better you?

_____

_____

_____

_____

_____

_____

_____

_____

_____

_____

_____

_____

_____

_____

_____

_____

_____

_____

_____

_____

_____

_____

_____

_____

_____

_____

_____

_____

_____

...HerStory

MEMOIRS FROM DAUGHTERS TO MOTHERS AS THEIR MENTORS

_____

_____

_____

_____

_____

_____

_____

_____

_____

_____

_____

_____

_____

3. What are the 9 steps that you will do for the next 30, 60, 90 days to help you achieve your next steps? What method will you use to track these steps?

_____

_____

_____

_____

_____

_____

_____

_____

_____

_____

_____

_____

_____

_____

_____

_____

_____

_____

_____

_____

_____

_____

_____

_____

_____

_____

_____

_____

_____

CHAPTER 9

FORGIVENESS! THE REASON WE SHOULD FORGIVE AND NEVER FORGET...

FORGIVENESS

We have all heard that we do not forgive others, but we forgive to make us better. This statement has never been truer than today. Our growth and happiness are vital to forging ahead in life. As we live through pain, hurt, resentment, and anger, it can hurt or stifle our growth. Forgiveness frees us to live in the present and to go forward, leaving the pain, hurt, resentment, and anger behind. There are benefits to forgiving those that have hurt us. The benefits include:

- Better health
- Better self-esteem
- Improved mental health
- Less alcohol use
- Less drug use
- Less hostility, stress, and anxiety
- Fewer symptoms of depression

In order for me to move forward into the future, it was important to let go of the grudges and bitterness and live in the now. As we work hard to forgive ourselves and then others, we will gain opportunities to repair relationships and become a better person.

Forgiveness is work. We must realize that although we forgive someone, we must never forget the lesson learned. As we forgive, we must also realize that everyone can't be a part of our journey. Forgiveness is for YOU and your personal growth. Forgive but never forget!

Questions

MEMOIRS FROM DAUGHTERS TO MOTHERS AS THEIR MENTORS

1. Who do you need to forgive to receive your blessings?

_____

_____

_____

_____

_____

_____

_____

_____

_____

_____

_____

_____

_____

_____

_____

_____

_____

_____

_____

_____

_____

_____

_____

_____

_____

_____

_____

_____

_____

_____

MEMOIRS FROM DAUGHTERS TO MOTHERS AS THEIR MENTORS

_____

_____

_____

_____

_____

_____

_____

_____

_____

_____

_____

_____

_____

_____

2. What steps will you take to remove the toxicity of unforgiveness in your life?

_____

_____

_____

_____

_____

_____

_____

_____

_____

_____

_____

_____

_____

_____

_____

_____

_____

_____

_____

_____

_____

_____

_____

_____

_____

_____

_____

_____

_____

_____

_____

_____

_____

_____

_____

_____

_____

_____

_____

_____

_____

_____

_____

_____

_____

_____

3. What are the 9 steps that you will do for the next 30, 60, 90 days to help you achieve your next steps toward forgiveness? What method will you use to track these steps?

_____

_____

_____

_____

_____

_____

_____

_____

_____

_____

_____

_____

_____

_____

_____

_____

_____

_____

_____

_____

_____

_____

_____

_____

_____

_____

_____

_____

_____

_____

_____

_____

_____

_____

_____

_____

_____

_____

_____

_____

_____

_____

CHAPTER 10

THE
NEXT CHAPTER...

DR. BLUE'S NEXT CHAPTER IN LIFE

"...HerStory" will be filmed, shared, and edited to continue the great work of mentorship. This book and the stories that are included are connected to the title of the book. The goal is to bring bright minds together to share a focus on our mothers as mentors to invoke learning, inspiration, and wonder to provoke conversations about our mothers as mentors to help other women that have or will encounter our particular situations. The stories in this book are included to intentionally influence the lives of others that read this book.

The next book will be dedicated to the girls becoming women entrepreneurs. Many of us wanted to be with our mothers, but life's circumstances forced us to lose them early or to be without them without our permission. As a result, the little girl in us longs for our mothers, dead or alive.

CHAPTER 11

HOW
CAN I
MAKE
A
DIFFERENCE?

YOU CAN MAKE A DIFFERENCE RIGHT WHERE YOU ARE

You can start by reading, ordering, and sharing this book with someone that needs to hear these stories.

If you would like to order additional copies of ...*HerStory* for your organization, business colleagues, friends, or family, call: Blue Pathways at 616-634-9362 or send an email to bluepathwaysmentorship@gmail.com.

Do You Have A Group To Train or Educate?

If you would like to attend a workshop on mentorship or ...*HerStory*, call us. Participants return with new tools, practical strategies, and powerful skills that enhance their effectiveness immediately.

You can schedule training where and when it is most convenient for you! We will train your group on-site at your location.

Plus, as an added value, we will customize the workshops to meet your organization's vision, mission, and objectives. With group training from Blue Pathways, you will receive MORE for LESS ...

- **More time** left for you – When you partner with us, you save time and money on the development, administration, and delivery ... we do the work; you receive the results—fast!
- **Less** turnaround time between pieces of training and a request to delivery
- **More focus** on the exact needs of your organization and your people
- **Less "nonspecific"** information
- **More positive change** when many associates absorb new ideas and learn new methods at the same time
- **Less chance** that people will miss out on learning
- **More value** for your training dollar – Our no-hassle curriculum licensing agreement means you can cascade the learning throughout your organization
- **Less total investment** per associate

If you are expected to do MORE with LESS, join the thousands of organizations that choose Blue Pathways for customized training. Call us at 616-634-9362 to discover how easy and cost-effective it is to partner with us.

NOTES...

...HerStory
MEMOIRS FROM DAUGHTERS TO MOTHERS AS THEIR MENTORS

_____

_____

_____

_____

_____

_____

_____

_____

_____

_____

_____

_____

_____

_____

MEMOIRS FROM DAUGHTERS TO MOTHERS AS THEIR MENTORS

_____

_____

_____

_____

_____

_____

_____

_____

_____

_____

_____

_____

_____

_____

_____

_____

Blue Pathways is here to Motivate, Educate, and Lead to take individuals beyond their today and into their tomorrow!

CHAPTERS REVISITED

All names in this book have been changed. In a few stories, minor changes have been made to protect the identity of the author.

Chapter 1: Humble Beginnings In Life

Chapter 2: Memories from A Young Age Can Cause Pain

Chapter 3: My Mother, My Rock

Chapter 4: My Past Is Not My Future

Chapter 5: Difficult Relationships Are Lessons Taught

Chapter 6: The Love of A Mother Conquers All

Chapter 7: Mothers Hurt Too

Chapter 8: Motherless Child

Chapter 9: Forgiveness

Chapter 10: Dr. Blue's Next Chapter in Life

Chapter 11: How Can I Make A Difference?

Notes

Need More Books

References

HOW TO
BOOK
DR. BLUE...

Feel free to book Dr. Blue for speaking engagements, team building activities, workshops, professional developments, and student assemblies at:

Website:

http://bluepathwaysmentorshipservices.com/

Facebook:

https://www.facebook.com/BluePathway/

Instagram:

https://www.instagram.com/bjenterprisesllc/?hl=en

LinkedIn:

https://www.linkedin.com/in/dr-andrea-b-70b6111a/

REFERENCES

Bettinger, E. P., & Baker, R. B. (2014). The effects of student coaching: An evaluation of a randomized experiment in student advising. *Educational Evaluation and Policy Analysis, 36*(1), 3-19.

Duppong-Hurley, K., Lambert, M. C., Epstein, M. H., & Stevens, A. (2015). Convergent validity of the strength-based behavioral and emotional rating scale with youth in a residential setting. *The Journal of Behavioral Health Services & Research, 42*(3), 346-354. doi:10.1007/s11414-013-9389-0

Fruiht, V. M., & Wray-lake, L. (2013). The role of mentor type and timing in predicting educational attainment. *Journal of Youth and Adolescence, 42*(9), 1459-72. doi:10.1007/s10964-012-9817-0.

George, M. P., & Sebastian, R. M. (2012). A model for student mentoring in business schools. *International Journal of Mentoring and Coaching in Education, 1*(2), 136-154. doi:10.1108/20466851211262879

Hasler, M. G. (2013). *Leadership development in context: A descriptive mixed method study of leadership development* activities during significant organizational change (Doctoral Dissertation). Retrieved from ProQuest Dissertations and Theses database. (305122914

Jones, S. M. (2014). Diversity leadership under race-neutral policies in higher education. *Equality, Diversity and Inclusion: An International Journal, 33*(8), 708-720.

Katherine, C. M., Welton, A., Pei-Ling, L., & Young, M. D. (2014). The lived experiences of female educational leadership doctoral students. *Journal of Educational Administration, 48*(6), 727-740. doi:10.1108/09578231011079584

Nordhagen, S., Calverley, D., Foulds, C., O'keefe, L., & Wang, X. (2014). Climate change research and credibility: Balancing tensions across professional, personal, and public domains. *Climatic Change, 125,* 149-162. doi:10.1007/s10584-014-1167-3

Scherdin, M., & Zander, I. (2014). On the role and importance of core assumptions in the field of entrepreneurship research. *International Journal of Entrepreneurial Behavior & Research, 20*(3), 216-236.

Talbert, P. Y. (2012). Strategies to increase enrollment, retention, and graduation rates. *Journal of Developmental Education, 36*(1), 22-24, 26-29, 31, 33, 36.

144

www.ingramcontent.com/pod-product-compliance
Lightning Source LLC
Chambersburg PA
CBHW031513040426
42445CB00009B/208